Unraveling the Mystery of the Blood Covenant

by
John Osteen

Copyright © John Osteen
P.O. Box 23117
Houston, Texas 77228

ISBN 0-912631-34-1

Contents

INTRODUCTION

For years I read books and heard sermons on the subject of the Blood Covenant between God and man, but failed to understand the full implications of what it meant. I wrestled with the subject, but could never quite comprehend the full significance of this important subject. I feel sure that if this happened to me, you may have struggled with it, too.

Some of the best teaching God has helped me do has come when I've taken some deep spiritual truth from God's Word and run it through my simple mind and heart, then brought it out on a level where ordinary people like me can understand it. In this book, I have tried to put the profound teaching of the subject of the Blood Covenant into simple language all of us can understand.

Your Christian experience will take on a breathtaking new meaning when you begin to grasp some of the marvelous things God has done for us through the power of the blood of the Lord Jesus Christ.

When you finish reading this book, don't put it away. I strongly advise you to read and reread it until its message settles way down deep in your understanding and moves your relationship with God into a higher dimension.

John Osteen

Chapter 1

The Mystery of Redemption

To understand God's plan of redemption, it is important to know that the Bible is made up of two covenants called the Old Testament and the New Testament. All of God's dealings with the human race have revolved around these two testaments. The entire redemptive plan of God hinges upon them. God established the first covenant with Abraham, and the second covenant with Jesus. It's as simple as that.

Testament means "covenant." And the word *covenant* comes from a verb meaning "to cut," suggesting an incision from which blood flows.

For years I preached on the covenant without knowing what the word actually meant. I didn't fully understand God's plan to use the covenant agreement to redeem mankind. Yet because of its original meaning, "covenant" is the strongest word a lawyer can use today to bind two parties to fulfill the obligations of an agreement.

Satan stole the human race from God

In the Garden of Eden, in the very beginning, Satan tempted the human race to disobey the Word of God. *God commanded the man, saying, Of every tree of the garden thou mayest freely eat: But of the tree of the knowledge of good and evil, thou shalt not eat of it: for in the day that thou eatest thereof thou shalt surely die* (Genesis 2:16,17).

First, Satan, deceived the woman, Eve, by talking her into partaking of the forbidden fruit, saying, *Ye shall not surely die* (Genesis 3:4). First Timothy 2:14 says, *And Adam was not deceived, but the woman being deceived was in the transgression.*

Romans 5:19 explains the original sin like this, *By one man's disobedience many were made sinners.* As a result of sin, the human race was imprisoned in darkness. Adam and Eve, who had actually had the very life of God—eternal life—inside them, now were members of the family of Satan. When they sinned, they passed out of light into darkness. Romans 6:16 says, *Know ye not, that to whom ye yield yourselves servants to obey, his servants ye are to whom ye obey; whether of sin unto death, or of obedience unto righteousness?*

When God created Adam, He gave him authority to rule and reign over all He had created. As long as Adam fellowshipped with God and obeyed His commands, he kept his authority.

The moment Adam sinned, he relinquished his authority to the devil. And Satan became the god of this present world system. God commanded Adam to have dominion on earth like God had in Heaven; but through Adam's disobedience, Satan became the god of this world (see 2 Corinthians 4:4). Satan usurped man's God-given authority and seized control of the human race.

You see, God operates by the laws set forth in His Word. God couldn't break His own laws and take back His creation.

Satan knew this, so he deceived Adam and Eve to gain legal authority over the whole human race. Every man, woman, and child from that time on has been born with a sin nature that has been passed down from Adam's sin. *Wherefore, as by one man* [Adam] *sin entered into the world, and death* [separation from God] *by sin; and so death passed upon all men, for that all have sinned* (Romans 5:12).

This is the reason you don't have to teach people to fear. They just naturally fear. You don't have to teach people to lie. They just naturally lie. You don't have to teach people to be unkind to one another. They are just naturally unkind to one another. You don't have to teach people to quarrel and fight. They just naturally quarrel and fight. This is because they are born with the nature of the devil. There is a demonic force on the inside of every lost man or woman, which the Apostle Paul referred to as *the spirit that now worketh in the children of disobedience* (Ephesians 2:2).

A mystery hidden in God

After Satan deceived Adam and Eve and took possession of the human race, the fellowship between God and man was broken. In order to restore that fellowship, God immediately set a plan in action to win back mankind. *Redemption* means "to buy back."

God never told the human race the details of His plan for their redemption. The Bible says even the prophets didn't understand what they prophesied about a coming Redeemer. They searched their own prophecies diligently, wondering what they meant. The devil didn't know what God was doing. The Apostle Paul wrote in 1 Corinthians 2:8, that if the princes of this world (that is, the demon powers) had known what was going on, they never would have crucified the Lord of glory. Redemption was a mystery hidden in God.

Abraham didn't know God's plan. He didn't understand that God had to retrieve His legal right to man from Satan. Abraham didn't know that God had to find a man to covenant with Him. He had to find a man who would obey Him no matter what the cost—a man who would take God at His Word and believe Him. Through that man, God would bring forth a nation. Through that nation, He would bring forth a family. And in that family, He would choose a woman through whom He would bring forth a Redeemer, the Messiah. *But when the fulness of the time was come, God sent forth his Son, made of a woman, made under the law, to redeem them that were under the law, that we might receive the adoption of sons* (Galatians 4:4,5). God would make a new covenant with this Messiah and redeem the human race. No one in the Old Testament understood that. It was a mystery.

Even Moses didn't understand God's plan of redemption, and this lack of knowledge led to his not being allowed to enter into the Promised Land. God used certain things as types and shadows to teach His people of the coming Messiah, the Christ, and He wouldn't allow anyone to interfere with His plan. You may remember that while in the wilderness, Moses struck the rock twice to bring forth water instead of once as God told him to do. The rock represented Christ, and by striking it twice, Moses, without realizing it, was telling the world that Jesus needed to be crucified twice.

God said, "No! Let all the world know forever that you made a mistake and, because of it, you'll not go into the Promised Land. My Son will be smitten only once."

Think about it. The angels didn't know what God was doing. The devil didn't know what He was doing. Man didn't know. Yet today you and I live in the light of God's marvelous work of redemption. We look back to the events of the Garden of Eden and we can understand what God was doing from the beginning.

Chapter 2

What the Blood Covenant Is

Let me explain what the Blood Covenant is. The most helpful information I've found is in E. W. Kenyon's little book, *The Blood Covenant*, and one by the same title from Dr. H. Clay Trumbull. Dr. Trumbull was editor of the *Sunday School Times* and wrote the *International Sunday School Lessons* years ago. I recommend that you read both of these books.

The Blood Covenant is based upon the oldest covenant rite known to the human family.

Primitive people from the beginning of time have practiced blood covenants in some form. They were common among the Indian tribes of America, and the custom is still practiced in many parts of the world today.

They are incorporated into many witchcraft rituals, and I'm told that even the Mafia in the underworld participates in blood covenants.

There are many reasons for a blood covenant. To those who practice it, there is no covenant more sacred. In a partnership, it is used to make sure that neither partner will take advantage of the other. Between friends, it is a symbol of love, devotion, and loyalty. Primitive tribes regularly participate in blood covenants. A weaker tribe uses it to insure that a stronger one will not destroy it.

Let me share a story that has helped me as much as anything to understand the significance of the Blood Covenant.

David Livingstone, the famous explorer, was the first great missionary to Africa. He stayed in the jungles so long that England, fearing he was dead, sent another explorer, Sir Henry Stanley, on an expedition to search for him. A young African man, educated in England, accompanied Stanley and his party as their interpreter.

In his books, Stanley tells how he set out through the rugged wilds in his search for Livingstone. The country was filled with uncivilized tribes, and Stanley's party was plagued with disease, starvation, and cannibals.

On one occasion, the expedition came to an impasse when they encountered a powerful, hostile equatorial tribe that had no desire to let them through. Stanley's party was outnumbered and he didn't know what he was going to do.

Finally, Stanley's young interpreter told him, "You're going to have to cut a strong covenant with these people."

"What do you mean, 'cut a covenant' with them?" Stanley asked. He didn't understand what the term meant.

The interpreter explained, "This is what you're going to have to do: First, the chieftain of the tribe

14

will choose a substitute to represent him, and you'll choose a substitute to represent you. The two substitutes will come together before a priest, who will cut the wrist of each one just enough to drip a few drops of their blood into a glass of wine. The wine will then be stirred and the bloods mixed. The cup will be handed to one man who will drink part of it. Then he will hand the cup to the second man, who will drink the remainder of the mixture, thereby uniting the parties in a blood covenant.

"Sometimes the two will rub their wrists together so their bloods mingle, or they will touch their tongues to each other's wounds to seal their covenant.

"After drinking the blood mixture, often the two parties will rub gunpowder in the wound on their wrists so they will be forever marked like a tatoo as a blood-covenant man."

The covenant between Stanley and the chief

The idea of a blood covenant was revolting to Stanley, but he knew their situation was desperate. So he agreed. After several days of negotiations, arrangements were made for the blood-covenant ritual. Stanley chose his interpreter to be his substitute, and the chief chose a prince as his substitute.

The two substitutes went through the blood-covenant rite while Stanley and the chief looked on. Both substitutes drank the blood mixture. Now, Stanley and the chief were blood brothers.

As soon as they finished, Stanley said, the priest stepped forward and pronounced the many blessings and good things the chief would now do for Stanley.

"Oh, that sounded good!" he said. Then, all of a sudden, the priest began pronouncing terrible curses upon Stanley.

"What is he doing now?" Stanley asked his interpreter. "Why is he cursing me?"

"He is pronouncing the curses that will come upon you if you ever dare break this covenant," he answered.

Stanley's interpreter then took his part and pronounced blessings upon the chieftain and his family and curses if he ever broke the covenant.

After the covenant was sealed in their blood, Stanley said a marvelous thing happened. The chief stood up and said, "Now, buy and sell with Mr. Stanley. He is our blood brother!"

"I never had to worry one moment about my goods any more," the explorer said. "Nobody would dare steal from me because I was in a covenant relationship with the chief and his tribe. Stealing from a blood brother carried a death penalty."

Stanley said he never knew a blood covenant to be broken in Africa. No man dared to break the covenant. If he did, his own family would turn him over to the hands of the avenger to be killed.

So sacred was the blood covenant that it was revered and kept by succeeding generations. It was a perpetual covenant that could not be broken or dissolved.

Chapter 3

What the Blood
Covenant Means

When a blood covenant is cut, it is often the custom for blood brothers to exchange gifts, symbolizing that everything one has is at the disposal of the other if he needs them.

Stanley suffered with stomach ulcers, and about the only nourishment he could take was goat's milk. He took a goat with him wherever he went all over Africa. It was his most prized possession.

When he and the tribal chief came to the gift exchange step of the covenant ritual, the chief requested Stanley's new white goat. He said to the interpreter, "Tell Mr. Stanley that since he is a blood brother, I want him to give me his best. And I see that the thing he prizes most is his goat. I'd like to have his goat."

Talk about getting your goat!

It was very difficult for Stanley to do, but the chief would have nothing else. So Stanley gave him his goat.

Then the chief brought his best gift and gave it to Mr. Stanley—a seven-foot spear, coiled with copper around it.

What will I ever do with this old spear? Stanley wondered. However, it wasn't long until he made a wonderful discovery. The chief's spear was known throughout the continent of Africa. It belonged to the chieftain of the most powerful tribe of the country. Wherever Stanley went with that spear everyone bowed to him.

"Why are they doing that?" he asked his interpreter.

"Because you are carrying the chief's spear. All you have to do is ask, and they will give you anything they have."

Stanley said, "I want a milk goat."

The natives gave Stanley a whole herd of milk goats!

Oh, what that spear represented! Lifted in the air, that spear opened up the darkest regions of the continent of Africa for Mr. Stanley because of the authority that was behind it. It said, "This belongs to the mightiest chief in all Africa." And the natives bowed their knees.

Not until then did Stanley fully realize the tremendous power of the blood covenant and what it meant. He reportedly used the rite at least fifty times with different tribes in his journeys in Africa.

Chapter 4

God's Covenant With Abraham

The rite of the blood covenant is the most enduring and most sacred pact known to man. There are historic traces of its widespread existence in every part of the world since time immemorial.

Now, you may be wondering where this idea came from in the heathen world.

It is evident that the idea of a blood-covenant relationship came from God. He revealed it to man in the very beginning. Many believe that God entered into a Blood Covenant with Adam and Eve in the Garden of Eden.

Did you know that all the heathen world have ideas about creation very similar to ours with Adam and Eve? They even have various stories of the flood. Dr. H. Clay Trumbull wrote that he believed the custom of "making brothers" to be of semitic origin and to have been introduced into Africa by heathen Arabs before the days of Mohammed.

The cutting of the covenant has been defiled and misused by many cultures. There are many differences in the rite, but its meaning is always the same.

God took the first step

When God approached a man named Abraham about a covenant, there was no harmony between God and the human race. Man had become the devil's offspring. And, like Mr. Stanley who went to the African chief, God took the initiative and sought to cut a covenant so He could have a restored relationship with man. It wasn't man's idea. It was God's.

Abram was 99 years old when God appeared to him, and said, *I am the Almighty God; walk before me, and be thou perfect. And I will make my covenant between me and thee, and will multiply thee exceedingly.*

And Abram fell on his face: and God talked with him, saying, As for me, behold, my covenant is with thee, and thou shalt be a father of many nations.

Neither shall thy name any more be called Abram, but thy name shall be Abraham; for a father of many nations have I made thee. And I will make thee exceeding fruitful, and I will make nations of thee, and kings shall come out of thee.

And I will establish my covenant between me and thee and thy seed after thee in their generations for an everlasting covenant, to be a God unto thee, and to thy seed after thee.

And I will give unto thee, and to thy seed after thee, the land wherein thou art a stranger, all the land of Canaan, for an everlasting possession; and I will be their God (Genesis 17:1-8).

Dr. Trumbull states that a characteristic of primitive blood covenants was that anyone who chose to enter such a covenant had to be ready to make a complete surrender of himself to the one with whom he covenanted. "He must, in fact, so love and trust, as to be willing to merge his separate individuality in the dual personality of which he becomes an integral part," he writes. (Dr. H. Clay Trumbull, *The Blood Covenant* [Kirkwood: Impact Books, Inc., 1975], pg. 220.)

Genesis 15:6 tells us that Abraham believed God and it was counted unto him for righteousness. The word "believe" here signifies that Abraham made a total commitment of himself and all that he had to God.

How God established the covenant with Abraham

When God wanted to establish His covenant with man, He had to have a sacrifice to represent Him. He said to Abraham, *Take me an heifer of three years old* (Genesis 15:9).

Notice, God said, "Take *for Me* a sacrifice." God was saying, "Abraham, I'm a party in the covenant that I'm going to establish with you. I'm a spirit being. I need somebody with two physical hands to take Me a sacrifice to be a substitute in My place."

Abraham did as God asked. He took an animal as God's substitute and shed its blood for Almighty God so that, in the sense realm, man could see and understand God's covenant with him.

Circumcision—the seal of the covenant

Then God explained to Abraham how he was to enter into the blood-covenant relationship:

This is my covenant, which ye shall keep, between me and you and thy seed after thee; Every man child among you shall be circumcised.

And ye shall circumcise the flesh of your foreskin; and it shall be a token of the covenant betwixt me and you (Genesis 17:10,11).

In other words, God said, "Abraham, My substitute has been slain. Now I want you to circumcise yourself by cutting off the foreskin, and let the blood flow. Let your blood mingle with the blood of My substitute. Through the act of cutting, My covenant will be in your flesh and we will be blood brothers. You will be a covenant-man, and you will be a friend of God."

I believe God asked Abraham to cut the covenant at the place on his physical body which represented the very source of life for himself and his seed. Thus when Abraham circumcised himself, he was pledging not only to unite himself, but also his descendants, to God.

God said, *He that is eight days old shall be circumcised among you, every man child in your generations, he that is born in the house, or bought with money of any stranger, which is not of thy seed.*

He that is born in thy house, and he that is bought with thy money, must needs be circumcised: and my covenant shall be in your flesh for an everlasting covenant (Genesis 17:12,13).

That very day Abraham and all the men of his house were circumcised (see Genesis 17:24-27). Forever after, Abraham bore in his flesh the evidence that he had entered into a blood-covenant relationship with Almighty God.

The seal of the covenant was circumcision. The covenant bound Abraham and his descendants to God with a tie that could not be broken, and God was bound to them by the same solemn token.

God's secret was still not known, but He was on His way to redeeming man. He was setting in action His plan which would guarantee that every daughter and every son that you and I have can go to heaven and not go to hell. Glory be to God!

The moment a covenant is officially completed, everything a blood brother owns is at the disposal of his blood brother.

Now God said, "Abraham, everything I have is at your disposal through the covenant. But, also, since you're in a blood relationship with Me, everything you have—your best—has to be at My disposal."

Chapter 5

Abraham's Supreme Test

Have you ever wondered why God asked Abraham to sacrifice his son, Isaac?

"He did it to test Abraham," you're probably saying.

You're right. He did. After the covenant was cut, God decided to test Abraham's allegiance to their covenant relationship.

Isaac was the son of promise, and Abraham prized Isaac's life far more than his own. This son of his old age was dearer than any possession he had on earth. Abraham and Sarah had waited many long, lonely years for a son. Isaac was the only hope Abraham had that God's promise to him would ever be fulfilled.

You remember, God's covenant promise to Abraham was that a whole nation would descend from him. He told Abraham, *As for Sarai thy wife, thou shalt not call her name Sarai, but Sarah shall her name be. And I will bless her, and give thee a son also of her: yea, I will bless her, and she shall be a mother of nations* (Genesis 17:15,16).

In the natural, God's promise for Sarah to bear a child was an impossibility. Abraham was almost 100 years old, and Sarah was 90. The Bible says, *Abraham and Sarah were old and well stricken in age; and it had ceased to be with Sarah after the manner of women* (Genesis 18:11). In spite of the circumstances, Abraham believed God. The Bible says that he considered not his own body, which was as good as dead, nor the deadness of Sarah's womb. He believed God could and would perform what He had promised (see Romans 4:19,20).

God was faithful to His Word. Genesis 21:1-3 says, *And the Lord visited Sarah as he had said, and the Lord did unto Sarah as he had spoken. For Sarah conceived, and bare Abraham a son in his old age...And Abraham called the name of his son that was born unto him, whom Sarah bare to him, Isaac* [which means laughter].

When the child grew to be a young boy, one day God said, "Now I'm going down to My blood brother, Abraham, the one who cut the covenant with Me, and test his faith and obedience. I will see how much he *really* loves Me."

God said, "Abraham, I've given you wealth and protection. I've given you everything you need. I've given you all that you've asked for. Now I'm going to ask for something—your best."

What was Abraham's best?

Isaac!

God said, *Take now thy son, thine only son Isaac, whom thou lovest, and get thee into the land of*

Moriah; and offer him there for a burnt offering upon one of the mountains which I will tell thee of (Genesis 22:2).

Abraham never batted an eye. He never hesitated. He said, "God, if you want Isaac, he's Yours."

When the Blood Covenant is in effect in your life and God tells you to do something, you don't hesitate. You do it.

The Word says that Abraham was willing to offer *up his only begotten son, of whom it was said, That in Isaac shall thy seed be called: Accounting that God was able to raise him up, even from the dead; from whence also he received him in a figure* (Hebrews 11:17-19).

When Abraham laid Isaac on the altar and lifted the glistening knife in the air to slay his son, the angel of the Lord called to him out of heaven, *Abraham, Abraham...Lay not thine hand upon the lad, neither do thou any thing unto him: for now I know that thou fearest God* [that God is first in your life], *seeing thou hast not withheld thy son, thine only son from me* (Genesis 22:11,12).

Abraham looked and saw that a ram was caught in a thicket for the sacrifice. God did not require Abraham to sacrifice his son, but He wanted Abraham to be *willing* to give Him his best.

God knew now that He had found a man who would keep the covenant, and God had respect for His covenant-man.

A covenant-keeping God

God said, *By myself have I sworn, saith the Lord, for because thou hast done this thing, and hast not withheld thy son, thine only son: That in blessing I will bless thee, and in multiplying I will multiply thy seed as the stars of the heaven, and as the sand which is upon the sea shore; and thy seed shall possess the gate of his enemies; And in thy seed shall all the nations of the earth be blessed; because thou hast obeyed my voice* (Genesis 22:16-18).

So immutable was God's promise that He said, "By myself have I sworn." God's very being, His throne itself, became the surety of His promise to man that He is a covenant-keeping God.

Abraham proved His faith in God by his actions, his works. He reminds us that our faith must be more than head knowledge. If our faith is not reflected in our actions, our words, and our behavior, it is not real faith.

The day Abraham was willing to offer up his only son, Isaac, James 2:23 says, *The scripture was fulfilled which saith, Abraham believed God, and it was imputed unto him for righteousness: and he was called the Friend of God.*

Abraham was now God's closest friend. And God gave fresh evidence to the closeness of their covenant relationship when He had to destroy Sodom and Gomorrah because of their wickedness. God couldn't just promiscuously wipe out those cities. He had a covenant-man down there He had to discuss the issue with. God said, *Shall I hide from Abraham that thing which I do…*(Genesis 18:17).

Oh, doesn't that do something to you? When you're a covenant-man or covenant-woman, God is not going to hide anything from you. We are not children of the darkness. We don't go around talking about preparing for calamity by hiding in the fields and digging holes in caves and storing food. We're covenant-men and covenant-women of God who know He is going to take care of us!

When God got ready to destroy Sodom and Gomorrah, He first went down and talked to His covenant-man and told him what He was about to do.

You know the story. Abraham pleaded with God brother-to-brother, friend-to-friend, for any righteous in the cities to be saved. On the basis of his blood-covenant relationship with God, Abraham became the intercessor between the wicked and God.

Because Abraham interceded, God saw to it that Abraham's relatives were rescued. He got his nephew Lot and Lot's wife and two daughters out of the doomed cities (see Genesis 18,19).

My friend, it may seem there is no hope in your situation—that your loved ones will never come to the Lord. But don't give up. Keep standing in the presence of God. Don't let the devil have your loved ones. Don't let them go to hell.

Like Abraham, you may be the only person who really cares enough to pray for them. You may be the only light in their dark world. So hold on. Don't give up on that dad, that mother, that son or daughter, no matter how far from God they have drifted.

If you will keep going before God and standing in His presence for them, I'm telling you that the God of Heaven who answers prayer will begin to work in their behalf, and one day you will shout for joy. You will see them delivered from the power of the devil and set free!

God respects the Blood Covenant. He could not and would not break the covenant because He is a covenant-keeping God. And He respects His covenant-keeping people.

Chapter 6

The Blessings of the Covenant

God cut the Blood Covenant with Abraham only. His descendants were included just by being circumcised. A child, by being circumcised, inherited all the blessings connected with the covenant.

Let me point out here that the key meaning of covenant is blessing. And Romans 11:17 tells us that you and I are grafted in like a wild olive tree to receive the same blessings God gave to Israel.

You remember that when Stanley's interpreter and the chief's prince cut the covenant, the priest stepped forward and pronounced both the blessings and curses that would accompany the covenant.

Similarly, in Deuteronomy 28, God pronounced the blessings that would come to those who fully walked in His ways and obeyed Him, as well as the curses on those who disobeyed. Here are just a few of the blessings of Abraham that belong to his descendants as a result of the covenant. These same promises belong to you. God said:

You will be blessed in the city and blessed in the country.

The fruit of your womb will be blessed, and the crops of your land and the young of your livestock — the calves of your herds and the lambs of your flocks.

Your basket and your kneading trough will be blessed.

You will be blessed when you come in and blessed when you go out.

The Lord will grant that the enemies who rise up against you will be defeated before you. They will come at you from one direction but flee from you in seven.

The Lord will send a blessing on your barns and on everything you put your hand to. The Lord your God will bless you in the land he is giving you.

The Lord will establish you as his holy people, as he promised you an oath, if you keep the commands of the Lord your God and walk in his ways. Then all the peoples on earth will see that you are called by the name of the Lord, and they will fear you (Deuteronomy 28:3-10, NIV).

Everything God's people touched would be blessed when they kept God's covenant. However, if they broke it, they would be cursed.

David understood the covenant

The covenant reached its zenith in David's day. Even as a young man, David must have understood the covenant, because when he went out to meet Goliath, the thing that astounded him was that this giant could defy the armies of the living God who were circumcised covenant-men.

When David visited his brothers in their encampment, he saw the thousands of soldiers in God's army quivering and shaking in the face of Goliath, because they either did not understand, had forgotten, or would not believe the truth of the Blood Covenant. But David, just a stripling of a youth, marched out to Goliath with the faith of God in him, and smote him.

David, a shepherd boy, had lain out under the stars on moonlit nights and thought about God—the God of Abraham, Isaac, and Jacob. He understood what it meant to be a covenant-man. When David saw the fear of the soldiers, he said, *Who is this uncircumcised Philistine, that he should defy the armies of the living God?* (1 Samuel 17:26).

What did David mean, "uncircumcised"?

He meant, "How dare this man who is not a covenant-man defy a man who is in a covenant relationship with God. Why," he said, "I bear in my body the mark of my unity with God. I am a covenant-man. I've shed my blood to enter into Abraham's covenant. Who is this uncircumcised giant to think he can harm us?

"Why, my covenant says that one shall chase a thousand, and two shall put 10,000 to flight. My covenant says that Almighty God has given me all His resources."

With that kind of faith, David marched out armed with a single slingshot and slew the mighty giant with a single rock, and brought victory to Israel.

When you read about the exploits of the mighty men of David's army, you realize they were covenant-men who understood that God would stand behind

His Word. They lived in the benefits of their covenant relationship with God.

God obligated himself

In his book, *The Blood Covenant*, E. W. Kenyon lists some of the things God obligated himself to do for those who lived in a covenant relationship with Him:

• God was under obligation to shield them from the armies of the nations that surrounded them.

• God was under obligation to see that their land brought forth large crops.

• God was under obligation by the covenant to see that their herds and flocks multiplied.

• The hand of God was upon them in blessing.

• They became the head of the nations and of wealth.

• Jerusalem became the richest city the world had ever known.

• Their hillsides were irrigated, their valleys teemed with wealth.

• There was no city like it, no nation like it. God was their God, they were God's covenant-people.

• Under the covenant, one man could chase a thousand in war, and two could put ten thousand to flight.

In David's day, when covenant truth became a living force in the nation, David had blood-covenant warriors that could individually slay eight hundred men in a single combat. They could, without weapons, rend a lion as though it had been a kid.

They had physical strength and prowess. They had divine protection that made them the greatest warriors the world ever knew. They were the treasure of the heart of God. (E. W. Kenyon, *The Blood Covenant* [Lynnwood: Kenyon's Gospel Publishing Society, 1969], pg. 28.)

For forty years, God, without a drugstore, a doctor, a prescription, or a clothing store, kept His covenant and preserved His people in the wilderness. Their shoes didn't wear out, and their clothes didn't get old. He fed them and gave them water to drink. He was their physician and kept them well and healthy by His divine power. Through astounding signs and wonders He brought His covenant-people out of Egyptian bondage and kept them as a nation.

Why? Because they had cut the covenant. Through substitutes, their blood had mingled with God's blood. They were God's covenant-people.

Israel breaks the covenant

Sadly, the time came when Israel sinned and broke the covenant. As a result, they brought destruction upon themselves. God lifted His hand of protection and they were carried away into Babylonian captivity, and the city of Jerusalem was destroyed.

When Israel sinned, God was faced with a dilemma. He had a choice—either kill them all or give them a sacrifice. So He gave them a sacrificial system. The only reason God instituted the sacrificial system was because they broke the covenant. He gave them a temporary way to stay in relationship with Him. When they sinned, instead of having the curse of sin come on them and dying, they could offer a sacrifice and be cleansed.

The sacrifices, laws, and priesthood of the Old Covenant were inadequate. However, through them, God was unfolding His mystery of a far better way. He was going to establish a New Covenant.

When you read the New Testament, especially the Book of Hebrews, in this light and substitute the word "covenant" for "testament," the revelation of the mystery will open up to you. Think of the new, the new, the new.

Behold, the days come, saith the Lord, when I will make a new covenant with the house of Israel and with the house of Judah (Hebrews 8:8).

Chapter 7

God's New Covenant
With Jesus

God remembered the covenant He had made
with Abraham years before. "Now," He said, "I'm
ready to cut a New Covenant with the house of Israel.
I will cut the New Covenant, not with Abraham, but
with the seed that I promised in the Garden of Eden—
with the Son of God who is going to appear through
the womb of a virgin. I cut the first covenant on the
physical level. Now I'm going to cut the New Covenant in the spiritual realm."

The Lamb of God
One day John the Baptist was preaching, and
there came to him a tall, rugged man, with rippling
muscles and a beauty that no man could describe. He
walked with stately grace. When John the Baptist saw
Jesus, he pointed to Him and said, *Behold the Lamb
of God, which taketh away the sin of the world* (John
1:29).

Remember when God cut the Old Covenant, He
told Abraham to take Him a sacrifice. Now God was

ready to cut the New Covenant, and again He needed a sacrifice, a lamb.

John said, "Behold the Lamb of God. In His veins course royal blood."

A baby gets its blood from the male sperm. God was Jesus' Father. Therefore, His blood was the blood of God, royal blood (see Acts 20:28). The Bible calls it "precious blood," "the blood of the everlasting covenant."

The Old Covenant was sealed by the blood of Abraham and the sacrificial animal. The New Covenant is sealed *with the precious blood of Jesus Christ, as a lamb without blemish and without spot* (1 Peter 1:19).

The first covenant was imperfect. It did not take away sin; it merely covered it up. It didn't give new life; it only gave the promise of it. The Old Covenant was like a promissory note which Christ cashed in on the cross of Calvary.

The Lord said He would make a New Covenant with Israel, *Not according to the covenant that I made with their fathers in the day when I took them by the hand to lead them out of the land of Egypt; because they continued not in my covenant, and I regarded them not, saith the Lord.*

For this is the covenant that I will make with the house of Israel [and with the Gentiles, which includes you and me] *after those days, saith the Lord; I will put my laws into their mind, and write them in their hearts: and I will be to them a God, and they shall be to me a people:*

And they shall not teach every man his neighbour, and every man his brother, saying, Know the

Lord: for all [who are in the covenant] *shall know me, from the last to the greatest.*

For I will be merciful to their unrighteousness, and their sins and their iniquities will I remember no more (Hebrews 8:9-12).

Jesus fulfilled the Old Covenant

God spoke of these new promises and this new agreement as taking the place of the old one. The Old Covenant was out of date now and had been put aside forever. Jesus fulfilled the Old Covenant. He said, *Lo, I come to do thy will, O God. He taketh away the first, that he may establish the second* (Hebrews 10:9).

The Apostle Paul explains the fulfillment of the Old Covenant through Jesus like this:

But Christ being come an high priest of good things to come, by a greater and more perfect tabernacle, not made with hands, that is to say, not of this building; Neither by the blood of goats and calves, but by his own blood he entered in once into the holy place, having obtained eternal redemption for us.

For if the blood of bulls and of goats, and the ashes of an heifer sprinkling the unclean, sanctifieth to the purifying of the flesh: How much more shall the blood of Christ, who through the eternal Spirit offered himself without spot to God, purge your conscience from dead works to serve the living God?

And for this cause he is the mediator of the new testament [covenant], *that by means of death, for the redemption of the transgressions that were under the first testament, they which are called might receive the promise of eternal inheritance* (Hebrews 9:11-15).

Paul continues to write:

Saying, This is the blood of the testament which God hath enjoined unto you. Moreover he sprinkled with blood both the tabernacle, and all the vessels of the ministry. And almost all things are by the law purged with blood; and without shedding of blood is no remission (vss. 20-22).

Christ entered into Heaven to appear before God for us as our Friend. He didn't have to offer himself again and again as the high priests did here on earth when they offered animal blood each year. Christ died once and for all to put away the power of sin forever by dying for us.

Jesus was God's Lamb, and through Him God cut an eternal covenant with the human race. Think about it. Hanging on the cross, suspended between Heaven and earth, Jesus took on himself all the sins of the world, all the sicknesses, all the diseases, all the suffering, all the heartbreak. He experienced the curse and the horror of all these dreadful things for us.

When Jesus died, He gathered up every sin from Adam and Eve to the last man and woman who will ever live on this earth—every transgression, every curse word, every act of adultery, every wicked thing man can do from the time of Adam and Eve to the end of the human race. Jesus saw it all, and He took it all into account. He took it all on himself for you and me.

Second Corinthians 5:19 says that God was in Christ, restoring the world to himself, no longer counting men's sins against them but blotting them out.

Every sin that man can ever commit has already been forgiven, erased, wiped out! They are covered with the blood of Jesus Christ. The good news is not that God *will* forgive you someday in the future. The good news is that He has *already* forgiven you. Now you only have to come to Christ and accept that forgiveness. The good news is not that God *will* reconcile us, but that He has *already* reconciled us unto himself. This is the wonderful message God has given us through the Blood Covenant.

When they stabbed Jesus in the side like a heifer, and the blood gushed out, God himself was cutting an everlasting covenant with the human race.

Again, He took the initiative just like He did when He cut the covenant with Abraham. He didn't wait for us. "Now," He said, "I have reconciled the world to Me. I have cut the covenant. I have shed My blood. I have done My part."

God has delivered us from the devil

Colossians 1:13 says that God has rescued us out of the darkness and gloom of Satan's kingdom and brought us into the kingdom of His dear Son.

God has broken the power of the devil, opened the prison doors, and delivered us out of Satan's power and kingdom. We don't have to serve him anymore.

There are so many who are in bondage to the devil today. They live in that dark kingdom, in the gloom of Satan's power. They have longed to be free, but they haven't heard the Good News. What is in that dark kingdom?—fear, torment, depression, poverty, misery, sickness, defeat—everything that hurts and destroys.

God has delivered us out of that kingdom of darkness and translated us into the kingdom of His dear Son. What a joy to be able to tell people that they don't have to stay in the prison house of the devil. They don't have to stay under the influence of drugs. They don't have to stay a prostitute, a gambler, a cheater, a liar. They don't have to stay with the filthy life that they've lived. They don't have to live with their broken homes and broken hearts.

If you are living in Satan's bondage, I want to tell you that you can go free! Satan has been defeated!

With the cutting of the New Covenant, God said, "Now everything I have is yours. I'll give you all I have. I'll make you heirs of God and joint-heirs with My Son, Jesus Christ."

The New Covenant is in Jesus

The Old Covenant was in Abraham; the New Covenant is in Jesus. When Abraham was circumcised, he mingled his blood with God's blood. Jesus shed His blood on the cross, mingling the human and the divine. All that God ever did in the Old Testament under the Old Covenant, He said He was doing for the sake of Abraham. What He does for us today, He does it for the sake of His Son Jesus.

You see, the New Covenant is not in us. It is in Jesus. God didn't cut the covenant with you and me. He cut it with His Son Jesus. I didn't realize this for a long time. It's important for you to understand this great truth.

Abraham proved his faith; therefore, his covenant was good. Jesus, our second Adam, can never fail. Jesus is unable to sin, unable to make mistakes, or break the covenant. He is the perfect man, ascended into the heavens, sitting at the right hand of God the Father, ever living to make intercession for us. He bears in His body the mark of the New Covenant.

He took the blood of the everlasting covenant beyond the stars and sprinkled it in the presence of the Father as an everlasting memorial that God has cut a New Covenant with me and with you.

How you enter the New Covenant

The Psalmist David had to enter into the covenant by circumcision. If David had refused circumcision, he wouldn't have been a covenant-man. We enter into the New Covenant today by circumcision. Not by the circumcision of the flesh, but by the circumcision of the heart, which is the new birth (see Romans 2:29). This is the cutting away of the old man of sin just like you cut away the superfluous flesh in physical circumcision and throw it away.

"Who can get in on this?" you ask.

Anybody who wants to can enter into the New Covenant. Now I didn't understand it at the time, but this is what happened when I got saved.

I was coming home from a dance in South Fort Worth, Texas, lost and undone, without God, when somebody told me about Jesus. I wasn't a covenant-man. I was a sinner.

You see, God knocked at my heart's door. Jesus had knocked on my door when I was a little boy and

43

said, "Did you know I've cut the covenant with the Father for you? Did you know the Father wants you? I've paid the price for your redemption. Did you know your sins have been forgiven? Did you know that you can have all that God has for you?"

I said, "No, Jesus, I don't want You."

Then He knocked again. I remember when He knocked, but I turned Him down.

That night when I was coming home from the dance, I couldn't resist. It seemed like Somebody walked beside me and began to knock and say, "Would you like to enter into the covenant with Me? Would you like to be circumcised in your heart and have all that God has for you? Would you like to have eternal life and be in covenant relationship with God? Would you like to be a covenant-man with God? Would you like to have all of God's resources at your disposal and have eternal life? And would you like to be God's man and be one with Him? I've cut the covenant for you. Would you like to get in on it by accepting Me as your Saviour?"

I didn't understand all God said to me that night. But I said, "Yes, I want You, Jesus." I didn't understand it in my head, but I understood in my spirit that I could have God's best. I had a right to God's best and would get it if I gave Him my best. And anything He ever wants or asks of me, if I'm a covenant-man, He has a right to ask me for it.

We get in on God's covenant blessings by circumcision of the heart. I was a lost man. I loved the world. I had an old man of sin that lived inside me, and I lived according to what he wanted to say and do. When I accepted Jesus, I was circumcised in my heart. The old man was cut away. And, I'll tell you, the angels rejoiced.

I can imagine somebody asking them, "Why are you rejoicing?" And they probably said, "We have another covenant-man, hallelujah! Somebody else has entered into the covenant that Jesus cut with the Father!"

A two-way commitment

Salvation is your coming to the place where you make an unqualified commitment to God. When Stanley and the African chief cut the covenant, they did it without any reservation. They were totally committed to each other and forever bound by their covenant.

I believe the reason some people walk down a church aisle and shake the preacher's hand but fail to get saved is because they don't really mean it. When you say, "God, I'm tired of sin, I'm tired of the world, I'm tired of burdens, and I don't want to go to hell. I make an unqualified commitment of everything I've got, spirit, soul, and body, to You. I want to be a covenant-man. I want Jesus. I want to get in on what He died for," God will save you!

When you become a covenant-person, God assigns angels to watch you and your family to see that no harm comes to you.

Then God says, "Angels, I charge you to watch after them and see that no calamity or plague comes nigh their dwelling. I charge you to bear them up in your hands lest they dash their foot against a stone. I charge you, Angels!" (See Psalm 91:11,12).

45

I want you to know that when you enter into a covenant relationship with God, He says, "Everything I have is yours. Everything I have is at your disposal."

I've had people say, "Brother Osteen, I wonder why God doesn't do anything for Me?"

God is looking for committed covenant-men and covenant-women. If God says, "Go to Africa," they say, "Tell me when." If God says, "Give that man your car," they answer "Yes, Lord." If God says, "Give $500 to My work," they respond, "Who do you want the check made out to, Lord?"

Everything we have belongs to God. It's at His disposal. And we're not to dispense it through sympathy. We're to be directed in our giving by Almighty God.

Jesus said when the Holy Ghost came, He would *glorify me: for he shall receive of mine, and shall shew it unto you. All things that the Father hath are mine; therefore said I, that he shall take of mine, and shall shew it unto you* (John 16:14,15).

When Jesus cut the covenant, everything God had belonged to Him, and He gave it to us. Paul wrote, *All things are yours; Whether Paul, or Apollos, or Cephas, or the world, or life, or death, or things present, or things to come; all are yours; And ye are Christ's; and Christ is God's* (1 Corinthians 3:21-23).

I believe that all God has is at my disposal. And I want to say it humbly, because I mean it from the depths of my heart, all that I have is at God's disposal.

Years ago, God asked me to go across this nation, and I said, "I'll go." He wanted me to go to the Philippines, and I said, "I'll go." He spoke to me to come back and pastor Lakewood Church, and I said, "I'll do it." Now, I'm waiting for His next call. God may allow me to pastor Lakewood Church until I die. But when He asks me to go any place, I want to be willing.

We have our home paid for. But if the Lord spoke to me, as He sweetly does sometimes, and said, "I want you to give your home to a certain couple," if I knew in my heart it was the Lord, I'd do it. And I know God. He would give me one back twice as big. God will never disappoint you, and you'll never go wrong by doing what God asks you to do.

A new breed

Just like God cut the covenant with Abraham to bring forth the nation of Israel, God cut the covenant with Jesus to bring forth a new holy nation, a peculiar people, zealous of good works (see 1 Peter 2:9 and Titus 2:14). We are not peculiar in dress or strange in behavior, but peculiar in that we are surrounded by the power of God. We walk in the Spirit of God. In Him we live, and move, and have our being.

Paul said, *Nevertheless I live; yet not I, but Christ liveth in me* (Galatians 2:20).

A new breed of people are arising today—people who, like David's soldiers, are covenant-men and covenant-women.

You remember how Stanley hated to give up his goat. Nevertheless, he led him over and gave him to the chief. And the chief gave him his wonderful spear.

One day, you and I took our old goat nature (we weren't lambs, but goats) and gave it to God. Oh, I

47

loved the world and all that was in it, and so did you. But we took our goat nature and gave it to our Chief, Jesus. In return, He gave us His Name to carry around with us. It is not the name of a church denomination—Baptist, Methodist, or Pentecostal—but the Name of Jesus. And, like the chief's spear, we found out that every knee in the regions of darkness bows to His Name.

When we march against the demonic powers of sickness, disease, poverty, and all the misery of mankind, all we have to do is lift the Spear—the Name of Jesus—and the demons say, "Huh oh, that's the Name of Jesus, the One who has conquered us." And they bow to that Name.

Jesus said, *Whatsoever ye shall ask in my name, that will I do, that the Father may be glorified in the Son. If ye shall ask any thing in my name, I will do it* (John 14:13,14).

It is in Jesus' Name, and His Name alone, that victory comes. It is not through our strenuous effort. It is not in our loud acclaim that we are strong. It is not through the knowledge we possess. It is not in anything that we have within ourselves. Only breathe the Name of Jesus, and it will do the work that needs to be done, for Jesus has cut the covenant for us.

Chapter 8

Understanding the Holy Communion

Jesus came to show us what God the Father is like and to introduce us to His love. John 3:16 says, *God so loved the world, that he gave his only begotten Son, that whosoever believeth in him should not perish, but have everlasting life*.

Jesus said, *As the Father hath loved me, so have I loved you: continue ye in my love* (John 15:9). There is no greater love than that which Jesus Christ portrayed for you and me on the cross of Calvary when He cut the New Covenant.

Jesus so loved us that He was willing to pour out His life blood to save us. The Communion is a love covenant, a love feast in which we affirm our love for God the Father, for Jesus, and for one another.

As we partake of the Lord's table, we are saying, "Jesus, I love You. Like the Father cut the first covenant with Abraham, You've cut the New Covenant for me in Your very own blood. And, Father, I love You, because You made it possible."

49

The bread represents the broken body of God's Lamb, Jesus Christ. The fruit of the vine represents the bleeding sacrifice and the covenant cut, Almighty God coming to our rescue through His Son Jesus. When you take these elements, you are saying, "Father, I freely accept the circumcision of my heart and my covenant relationship with You. All You have is mine, and all I have is Yours."

How grieved the Lord must be when we partake of the elements of the Holy Communion without understanding what we are doing. This is the reason 1 Corinthians 11:29 says we eat and drink "unworthily," or in an unworthy manner. Because we partake of the cup and the bread without understanding the meaning of what we are doing, the Bible says, many are weak and sickly among us, and many have died early deaths, not discerning the Lord's body. Only those who have been circumcised in heart and who discern what Jesus has done for us through the Blood Covenant, should partake of the sacrament of the Holy Communion.

I have been told by qualified authorities that in Jesus' day when the Jewish Passover was observed, three glasses were turned up, ready for wine to be poured in, and one was turned upside down. The three turned-up glasses were for Abraham, Isaac, and Jacob. The fourth, turned-down glass was for the Messiah.

When Jesus partook of the Passover meal with His disciples, He first passed the three glasses representing Abraham, Isaac, and Jacob. Then He turned up the one for the Messiah, signifying He had come, and poured in the fruit of the vine. He said to them:

With desire I have desired to eat this passover with you before I suffer: For I say unto you, I will not any more eat thereof, until it be fulfilled in the kingdom of God. And he took the cup, and gave thanks, and said, Take this, and divide it among yourselves: For I say unto you, I will not drink of the fruit of the vine, until the kingdom of God shall come.

And he took bread, and gave thanks, and brake it, and gave unto them, saying, This is my body which is given for you: this do in remembrance of me. Likewise also the cup after supper, saying, This cup is the new testament [the new covenant] *in my blood, which is shed for you* (Luke 22:15-20).

Jesus told His disciples He had looked forward with longing to the time when He could eat the Passover meal together with them. Then He lifted His glass and said, "This fruit of the vine represents the flowing of the cut from My body, which will take place shortly. It represents the blood of the New Covenant I am cutting for you."

Then Jesus took a loaf of bread, gave thanks, and broke it apart and gave it to them, saying, "This is My body which I give for you."

The old Blood Covenant was the foundation on which the New Covenant was established. When Jesus said, "This cup is the New Testament in My blood, which is shed for you," the disciples knew exactly what it meant. They knew that when they took the elements of the Communion with Jesus that night, they were entering into the strongest, most sacred covenant in existence. And this is what we must understand when we take Communion.

A covenant of love

The Communion also emphasizes our covenant relationship with all God's people. When you take communion, not only are you in loving covenant relationship with God but also you are in a love relationship with all of your brothers and sisters in Christ who partake with you.

Jesus said, *A new commandment I give unto you, That ye love one another; as I have loved you, that ye also love one another. By this shall all men know that ye are my disciples*, [My covenant-people], *if ye have love one to another* (John 13:34,35).

Love is what the Blood Covenant is all about.

Chapter 9

What the Blood of Jesus Christ Says to You

Did you know that the blood of Jesus Christ speaks to us? The Bible says it does.

Hebrews 12 tells us that we don't have to come to Mount Sinai that burned with fire and face terror as did the Israelites when God gave them His laws. They heard an awesome trumpet blast and heard a voice with a message so terrible that the people begged God to stop speaking.

That was under the Old Covenant.

How much different it is under the New Covenant. Now, the Word says, *Ye are come unto mount Sion, and unto the city of the living God, the heavenly Jerusalem, and to an innumerable company of angels, to the general assembly and church of the firstborn, which are written in heaven, and to God the Judge of all, and to the spirits of just men made perfect,*

And to Jesus the mediator of the new covenant, and to the blood of sprinkling, that SPEAKETH better things than that of Abel (vss. 22-24, emphasis mine).

The blood speaketh! But what does the blood say?

[It] *speaketh better things than that of Abel.*

When Cain killed Abel, God asked him, "Where is your brother, Abel?"

Cain answered, "How do I know? Am I my brother's keeper?"

God said, *The voice of thy brother's blood crieth unto me from the ground* (Genesis 4:10).

The blood of Abel cried out to God for vengeance, but the blood of Jesus Christ speaks better things than the blood of Abel. Thank God, where the blood of Abel cried out for vengeance, the blood of Jesus Christ cries out for mercy. Mercy! The blood of Jesus cries out to God on our behalf.

There are eight things the blood of Jesus Christ says to us. Let's look at them:

> One: You are justified.

Romans 5:9 says, *Being now justified by his blood, we shall be saved from wrath through him.*

The blood of Jesus Christ cries out, "You are justified!"

Justified is a theological term that not many people understand. But it means the same as "acquitted, declared innocent, not guilty." We all understand that.

When you go into a court of law, a jury hears all the evidence of the case being tried. Then they ponder and weigh the evidence and come back and bring the judge a verdict. Their verdict will say either *guilty* or *not guilty.*

That is what happened at Calvary. There, a great court session was held for the human race. We had a favorable position because God, the Judge, was our Father, and the Lawyer was our Savior, the Lord Jesus Christ. The jury brought in the verdict for all who accept Jesus into their hearts—*not guilty!*

We have been acquitted. Not because we were not guilty, but because Somebody paid our penalty. Jesus died in our place.

Romans 6:23 says, *The wages of sin is death; but the gift of God is eternal life through Jesus Christ our Lord.*

Two: You are redeemed.

Ephesians 1:7 says, *In whom we have redemption through his blood, the forgiveness of sins, according to the riches of his grace.*

The blood of Jesus cries, "You are redeemed!"

Many times when we want to approach God, the devil hurls his accusations at us and reminds us of our past. But the blood of Jesus speaks, "Redeemed! Redeemed! Redeemed!"

First Peter 1:18,19 says, *Ye were not redeemed with corruptible things, as silver and gold...but with the precious blood of Christ, as of a lamb without blemish and without spot.*

Jesus' blood cries, "You are redeemed!" The question is, from what are we redeemed?

Galatians 3:13,14 says, *Christ hath redeemed us from the curse of the law, being made a curse for us: for it is written, Cursed is every one that hangeth on a tree: That the blessing of Abraham might come on the*

Gentiles through Jesus Christ; that we might receive the promise of the Spirit through faith.

Read Deuteronomy 28 and you will find the list of curses—terrible dark things—that afflict and torment the human race because of sin. But the blood of Jesus says you have rights.

The blood of Jesus Christ that is sprinkled in the high court of Heaven gives you a right to be free from the miseries, the poverty, the pain, the sickness, and the disease which sin brought on this world. You have victory over these curses in the Name of Jesus, in whom we have redemption through His blood.

> Three: You have peace.

Colossians 1:20 says, *And, having made peace through the blood of his cross, by him to reconcile all things unto himself...*

The blood of Jesus speaks of what you have, and it says, "You have peace."

The thing men and women want more than anything else is peace. You can have all the gold and silver in the world, but if you don't have peace, you're miserable.

Do you know why people drink liquor? Why they get hooked on drugs? Why they live immoral lives? They are trying to find peace. But peace is not in a liquor bottle. It's not in drugs. It's not in illicit sex. It's not in wild living. It's in the blood of the Lord Jesus Christ.

Oh, peace is beyond the price of all money. Thank God, through the blood of Jesus Christ, we have peace *with* God and we have the peace *of* God.

You may be thinking, *But Brother Osteen, the Bible says God is angry with the wicked every day*.

Yes, the Old Testament says that, and He was. But the good news is that God has made peace with the human race. Jesus made it possible for man to come into that peace. That's good news!

If there's any reason this ministry has grown, other than because we teach the Bible, it's because we proclaim God's kindness to sinners. When we started out, I told the people to go out and find the prostitutes, the drunkards, the alcoholics, the drug addicts, the businessmen who are down and out, those who are crushed and hurting, the divorced, and those with broken lives. We invited them to come to church, and when they came, I didn't beat them over the head with sin and judgment. I told them of God's wonderful kindness.

The world is hungry to hear the Good News, but we have preached hell hot, sin black, and judgment sure. Sinners already have enough of that inside them. We are not to preach the problem; we are to preach the solution. Nobody wants to go to church and let you beat them over the head and grind them down to the ground about their problems. They go to church with a desire to hear a solution—His Name is Jesus.

It's not good news to go out and tell the world that God is mad at them. God is not mad. He loved the world so much He sent Jesus to die that they might be at peace with Him.

"Why, then, doesn't everyone have peace?" you ask. "Why doesn't everyone get saved?" These questions remind me of a conversation I had with my wife, Dodie.

One day Dodie was looking over her new book, *Healed of Cancer*, and she asked, "John, why did God decide to heal me when so many others have died of cancer?"

I said, "Dodie, God didn't choose to heal just you. God has chosen to heal everybody."

"Well, why was I healed?" she asked.

I said, "Because you decided to take God at His Word."

God doesn't play favorites. He is not a respecter of persons. Healing is for everyone. And salvation is for everybody. But you have to accept them. We have peace with God, because He made peace. Jesus didn't *bring* peace. He *made* peace. He made it by taking away the very thing that caused the war between God and man. And that was man's rebellion in sin. He took away the sin of the world.

The blood of Jesus does not say God *will* forgive you. It says God has *already* taken the initiative and forgiven you.

The gift of peace with God through Jesus' blood is a gift God has given to man. It is laying on the doorstep of the world, ready to be taken.

Four: You are God's property.

Hebrews 13:12 says, *Wherefore Jesus also, that he might sanctify the people with his own blood, suffered without the gate.*

The blood of Jesus says, "You are sanctified." In some denominations, people are always trying to "get sanctified." Thank God, I know I'm already sanctified by the blood of Jesus.

"Sanctified" is also a dense theological term that most of us don't understand. But, in simple terms, it means you are set apart for God's use. You are God's property.

The Word says you belong to God. *What? know ye not that your body is the temple of the Holy Ghost which is in you, which ye have of God, and ye are not your own? For ye are bought with a price: therefore glorify God in your body, and in your spirit, which are God's* (1 Corinthians 6:19,20).

When the devil tries to defeat you, the blood of Jesus cries out, "Take your hands off. That's God's property!" You see, when you give your heart to Jesus Christ and enter the New Covenant, you belong to God. You are set apart as God's property by the blood of Jesus. You are sanctified by His blood.

Five: You have eternal salvation.

Hebrews 13:20,21 says, *Now the God of peace, that brought again from the dead our Lord Jesus, that great shepherd of the sheep, through the blood of the everlasting covenant, make you perfect in every good work to do his will, working in you that which is well-pleasing in his sight, through Jesus Christ; to whom be glory for ever and ever.*

The blood of Jesus Christ says, "You have eternal salvation."

Through the blood of the everlasting covenant, you have an everlasting salvation. You are not going to go to heaven for 10,000 years, and then have your relationship with God run out. You have an *everlast-*

ing covenant with God. You have *eternal* redemption through the blood of Christ.

Six: You are cleansed.

First John 1:7 says, *But if we walk in the light, as he is in the light, we have fellowship one with another, and the blood of Jesus Christ his Son cleanseth us from all sin.*

The blood of Jesus says, "You are clean."

Thank God, when we make a mistake, we have hope. All we have to do is to confess that we have sinned—and confess that we are wrong—the blood of Jesus washes away our sin. The blood cries, "Clean!"

Have you ever had days when you were irritable all day? You went to church that night and you felt burdened down with guilt. You thought, *If everybody here knew how I've acted, they wouldn't want to have anything to do with me.*

There have been times when I've gone into the pulpit to preach and I felt so unworthy. The devil would say, "You're no good." But I've looked him in the eye and said, "Devil, you're a liar. The blood of Jesus Christ cleanses me. I'm free of the guilt of sin."

Seven: You are washed.

Revelation 1:5 says, *Unto him that loved us, and washed us from our sins in his own blood...*

The blood of Jesus Christ cries out, "You are washed!"

I love that old hymn, "Are You Washed in the Blood?" One verse says it all:

Lay aside the garments that are stained with sin,

And be washed in the blood of the Lamb;
There's a fountain flowing for the soul unclean,
O be washed in the blood of the Lamb.
Jesus' blood has already washed away our sins.

Eight: You have victory.

Revelation 12:11 says, *And they overcame him by the blood of the Lamb, and by the word of their testimony; and they loved not their lives unto the death.*

The blood of Jesus says, "You have victory!"

After you become a covenant-person, Revelation 12:11 takes on new meaning. It tells you how you can overcome the devil. You overcome him by three things:

First, by the blood of the Lamb. When the devil comes against you, hold up your Bible and say to him, "Devil, I want you to see this. This is God's everlasting Blood Covenant that Jesus cut for me. Christ's righteousness has been imparted to me. All God's power and blessings are mine. I command and charge you, Satan, look at that blood. You are already defeated."

Second, by the word of their testimony. You can boldly say, "Satan, I dare to stand on God's promises. It is written.... They are tried and proven. I'm a covenant-person, and God will not break His Word with me."

Third, they loved not their lives unto the death. These Christians made an unqualified commitment to God. All God had was theirs, and all that they had was His. They were covenant-men, covenant-women. They were willing to even sacrifice their own lives, if necessary, to live for Jesus and tell others about His way of living.

You don't overcome Satan by your tenacity. You don't overcome him by your good works. You don't overcome him by your goodness. You don't overcome him by your own holiness or righteousness. You don't overcome him by your mental agility. You overcome him by the blood of Jesus Christ.

Just present that blood to Satan and say, "See the blood, devil. The One who shed this blood crushed your head and took your power. He's my Lord!"

Yes, the blood of Jesus Christ speaks to you today. It cries out—

You are justified.

You are redeemed.

You have peace.

You are God's property.

You have eternal salvation.

You are clean.

You are washed.

And you have victory.

Oh, the wisdom of God, and the greatness of His wisdom! How unsearchable are His ways! How mighty is His wisdom for the human race and His love for man!

Chapter 10

The Big Question

Thank God for the blood of Jesus! Nothing else in this world—no good act, no prayer, no suffering, no sacrifice—can ever take away one of our sins. The only thing that will blot out sin is the blood of Jesus Christ.

God said, *I have blotted out, as a thick cloud, thy transgressions, and, as a cloud, thy sins* (Isaiah 44:22).

That verse of scripture used to worry me. Before we got all these newfangled ballpoint pens, we used ink fountain pens. If you spilled a little drop of ink, you blotted it. However, if you didn't do it carefully, the ink would smear and the spot would look worse than before.

When I read that God said He would blot out our transgressions, I thought, *Dear me, He's going to make it look worse than ever. He's going to make all these things I've done wrong really show up.*

Then I saw something in the rest of that verse. God said, "I have blotted out, *as a thick cloud*, thy transgressions." Have you ever seen the rays of the sun burn through a thick cloud of fog? The sun shines and shines until the cloud breaks up and suddenly just disappears. You can't find it. That's what happens to your sins. They cannot be found. God said, *I will be merciful to their unrighteousness, and their sins and their iniquities will I remember no more* (Hebrews 8:13).

What are you going to do with the blood of Jesus? That's the big question.

Exodus 12 tells the story of the Passover. God told the Israelites to kill a lamb without blemish and sprinkle its blood on the doorposts and over their doors. He was sending His death angel through the land of Egypt to execute judgment against all the gods of Egypt.

God said, *The blood shall be to you for a token upon the houses where ye are: and when I see the blood, I will pass over you* (Exodus 12:13).

Today, God is looking for the blood of Jesus Christ. If He sees it over your heart, then He says, "I will pass over you."

God is not looking for church membership. He's not looking to see whether you took the Lord's Supper or not. He's not looking for your mode of baptism. He's not looking for your good works. He said, "When I see the blood, I will pass over you."

Lots of people say, "I live a good life. I live by the Golden Rule. I try to treat others right. I'm an honest, hard-working person. I have good works. Maybe I'll be saved."

You cannot be saved by your good works. Jesus said, *Ye must be born again* (John 3:7). He said,

Except a man be born again, he cannot see the kingdom of God (vs. 3). That is, your inner man must undergo a radical change, which is called the new birth.

When you confess your sins and ask Jesus to come into your life, you become a new person. *Therefore if any man be in Christ, he is a new creature: old things are passed away; behold, all things are become new* (2 Corinthians 5:17).

Everything about you becomes new. Your way of thinking, your life-style, your behavior. The drunkard is no longer a drunkard. The blasphemer is no longer a blasphemer. The thief is no longer a thief. And the prostitute is no longer a prostitute. You are a new creation. The blood of Jesus makes this possible.

I don't care how much the devil has pulled you down, how many sins you've committed, how many blasphemous words you've spoken, how many adulterous acts you've committed, how many murders you've committed, how stained you are with sin. When you come to Jesus and accept Him, redemption makes you a new creation. There's not even the smell of your past in your spirit.

Your sinful past is no more. There's not any record of it. You become the righteousness of God. And the minute that happens, you become Satan's master. Every demon force is subject to you.

God has provided for His new creation to live victoriously

The very moment you believe on Jesus, you actually become part of a new race, a new species of people. Jesus was the firstborn among many brethren (see Romans 8:29), and every person who is born into the family of God after Him becomes part of this new race. It's a totally new race—a God-race. As the Lord and Head of this new kind of people, Jesus has provided that they can live victoriously.

Maybe you have never experienced the new birth. You have never been circumcised in your heart, and you would like to be. The Word says, *That if thou shalt confess with thy mouth the Lord Jesus, and shalt believe in thine heart that God hath raised him* [Jesus] *from the dead, thou shalt be saved* (Romans 10:9).

You can be saved and become a covenant-man, covenant-woman, or covenant-child right now. Just pray this prayer with me:

"Dear Father, I know that without Jesus I'm lost. Without Your Son, I'll die and go to hell. And, God, I don't want to be lost. I want to be saved. I want to go to Heaven.

"Now, Father, I turn away from the way I've been living, and I say, "Jesus, You're the Son of God, alive from the dead. You have already cut the New Covenant for me. Right now, I bring you my old goat nature and my sins to You and ask You to take them. I give them to you, Jesus, and I accept Your forgiveness. Come into my heart. Be my Lord. Be my Master. Be my Saviour.

"Now, devil, get out of my life. I'll serve you no more. I don't belong to you. I'm now God's Property. I am a child of God. Jesus is my Lord. I'm saved and my sins are gone, washed in the blood of Jesus. I'm redeemed. I'm declared not guilty. I've got eternal life. Thank God, I'm saved."

"In Jesus' name, I pray. Amen."

BOOKS BY JOHN OSTEEN

A Miracle for Your Marriage
Believing God for Your Loved Ones
Healed of Cancer by Dodie Osteen
How To Claim the Benefits of the Will
How To Demonstrate Satan's Defeat
How To Flow in the Super Supernatural
How To Release the Power of God
Overcoming Hindrances to Receiving the Baptism in the
　　Holy Spirit
Pulling Down Strongholds
Reigning in Life as a King
Rivers of Living Water
Six Lies the Devil Uses to Destroy Marriages by Lisa Osteen
The Believer's #1 Need
The Bible Way to Spiritual Power
The Confessions of a Baptist Preacher
The Divine Flow
The 6th Sense . . . Faith
The Truth Shall Set You Free
There Is a Miracle in Your Mouth
This Awakening Generation
Unraveling the Mystery of the Blood Covenant
What To Do When the Tempter Comes
You Can Change Your Destiny

MINIBOOKS

A Place Called There
ABC's of Faith
Deception! Recognizing True and False Ministries
Four Principles in Receiving From God
How To Minister Healing to the Sick
How To Receive Life Eternal
Keep What God Gives
Love & Marriage
Receive the Holy Spirit
Saturday's Coming
What To Do When Nothing Seems to Work
Selected titles also available in Spanish

Please write for a complete list of prices in the John Osteen Faith
Library Catalog. MANNA magazine is also available upon
request, free and postage paid.

John Osteen Ministries
P.O. Box 23117
Houston, Texas 77228